BEGINNING
WRESTLING

Photography by
Bruce Curtis

Thomas Ryan
Head Wrestling Coach, Hofstra University
& Julie Sampson

Sterling Publishing Co., Inc.
New York

This book is dedicated to all athletes who enjoy the thrill of sports — especially Jordan, Jake, Teague, MacKenzie, Troy, and Sheila Mae.

Thank you to Tom Brands, Terry Brands, Kendall Cross, and Vickie Zummo for taking the time to be interviewed for this book. Special thanks to Rob Anspach, Roman Fleszar, Dennis Papadatos, and the Elite Wrestling Club members.

Designed by Judy Morgan. Edited by Isabel Stein.
Photo on page 7 by Tom Ryan. Photo on page 25 courtesy of Vickie Zummo.

Library of Congress Cataloging-in-Publication Data

Ryan, Thomas (Thomas S.)
  Beginning wrestling / Thomas Ryan & Julie Sampson; photography by Bruce Curtis.
p. cm.
  Includes index.
  ISBN 0-8069-4625-3
    1. Wrestling—Juvenile literature. 2. Wrestlers—Juvenile literature [1. Wrestling. 2. Wrestlers.] I. Sampson, Julie. II. Curtis, Bruce, ill. III. Title.

GV1195.3 .R93 2001
796.812—dc21   2001020645

10 9 8 7 6 5 4 3 2 1

Published by Sterling Publishing Company, Inc.
387 Park Avenue South, New York, N.Y. 10016
© 2001 by Thomas Ryan and Julie Sampson
Distributed in Great Britain and Europe by Chris Lloyd at Orca Book Service,
Stanley House, Fleets Lane, Poole, BH15 3AJ, England
Distributed in Canada by Sterling Publishing
% Canadian Manda Group, One Atlantic Avenue, Suite 105
Toronto, Ontario, Canada M6K 3E7
Distributed in Australia by Capricorn Link (Australia) Pty Ltd.
P.O. Box 704, Windsor, NSW 2756, Australia
Printed in China
All rights reserved

Sterling ISBN 0-8069-4625-3

CONTENTS

Throughout this book there are helpful quotes from people who have found success through wrestling, including Tom Brands, Terry Brands, and Kendall Cross — who have won Olympic medals for the United States — and Vickie Zummo, an accomplished woman wrestler. These wrestlers offer their insights on wrestling, which can serve as great inspiration to you.

Wrestling is a sport for everyone. We hope this book not only informs you of the basic skills needed to find success on the mat, but also inspires you, no matter what your age and ability.

In gymnasiums all over the world, athletes of all sizes and abilities are drawn to wrestling for the simple reason that it is fun. It is a sport that tests the strength, stamina, and skill of two opponents. Wrestling is a physical chess match featuring moves and countermoves, endurance, strength, intelligence, and quickness. In wrestling, the opponents are of the same weight, so size is not an element in any wrestler's success.

For a beginning wrestler, it is crucial to learn the basics with correct form and technique. These basics are used at all levels of competitive wrestling.

The best way to get started in wrestling is to read through this book to gain an understanding of what the sport is about. Then call the local schools, parks, and libraries to find out what organized youth wrestling programs are in your area — for example, Police Athletic Leagues and town or city leagues. Wrestling is a tough sport, but if you work hard you can be successful.

GOALS AND ROLES 1

hildren as young as age four can begin to learn wrestling. There is no upper age limit at which an athlete should stop being involved in wrestling. Many people use wrestling as a means of staying physically fit and flexible throughout their lives (Photo 1).

A SAFE SPORT

Although it is a physically demanding sport, wrestling is one of the few activities that matches competing athletes according to their weights, which makes it a very safe sport. All wrestling is done on a mat that is cushioned to absorb falls during practice and competition. If you haven't already had a physical checkup for school, be sure to get a doctor's checkup before you start wrestling. Wrestling is a strenuous sport and it's important to get this go-ahead before starting. *Note to Parents and Coaches:* As youngsters begin to learn the basics, the most important thing that

1. Wrestling is a great sport for athletes of all ages.

coaches and parents should focus on is success through fun. Once the athlete gets good at the sport, he or she will gain respect from peers and will most likely want to pursue more competitive levels of the sport.

SETTING GOALS

It is important for you to make realistic goals for your current skill level. All wrestlers learning the basic skills must focus on using correct form (Photo 2). If you are just beginning, making it your

2. Two young wrestlers at practice.

goal to attend all practices and to concentrate during the whole practice is a good commitment. If you are a more experienced athlete, perhaps attempting to wrestle in a few club tournaments during the season would be a valuable experience — not for the sake of wins and losses, but to put some skills to the test in a live situation and to learn from the experience. Once you reach the junior high, high school or college level, it is a good time to discuss your personal goals with the local coach and your parents.

The more advanced you get in this sport, the more you must look at where you fit in the overall wrestling society. You should begin to ask yourself: "How willing am I to make the necessary sacrifices that go with training, nutrition, and competition?"

Whether you are a beginner or an experienced wrestler, it is important to know that success is learned in the wrestling room (Photo 3). Always remember that anyone can be a state champion!

3. Working hard in the wrestling room during practice helps all wrestlers become the best they can be.

If you are disciplined and work on improving personal weaknesses, success will be met. If finishing single-leg takedowns is a problem area for you, put in the time to work on that one weakness until it is mastered.

As a student of the sport, you must be eager to learn. When you go into a workout, your mind set should be: "I'm going to learn something in this workout. I will better myself as a wrestler today." Find ways to make the workouts interesting. Talk to other wrestlers and ask how they work out, or watch videotapes of competitions (Photo 4). Concentrate on all positions, including the top, bottom, and neutral positions.

As a beginning wrestler, you should not focus on winning and losing. The focus must be on learning. Set a plan for the day, the week, the month, and the season and try to meet those personal goals by taking one workout at a time. A coach or a parent should make sure that it is all kept interesting and fun for you, so that those goals can be reached.

4. Olympic gold medalist Tom Brands (bottom) teaches technique about the bottom position at a wrestling club clinic.

THE ROLE OF PARENTS

TOM AND TERRY BRANDS

Behind many successful wrestlers are parents who have been very supportive through it all. Olympic wrestlers Terry and Tom Brands both praise their parents for their constant support while they pursued their wrestling endeavors.

"My dad has an unbelievable mentality. He tells you like it is," Terry Brands says, "and that's how it is in wrestling. If you want something, then you have to go get it. The hardest part is actually doing it. That's where parental support is important."

Both Brands brothers agree that the desire to compete and succeed must come from within each wrestler. "Parents should not push with what they want their kids to do. When it comes to drilling and working out, the athlete has to do it, not the parents saying, 'Okay, now it's time to run,' or, 'Hit the weight room,' Terry Brands says. "I have seen kids being pushed by parents and they have succeeded in high school, but once they went away to college the self-discipline wasn't there because they never developed it on their own."

Terry Brands notes that there is a delicate balance between how involved a parent should get in the child's wrestling and how much a parent should back off. "Support is very important. The biggest thing is that if your child gets beaten, you can't yell at him or get down on him. He feels bad enough as it is. He's doing the best that he can."

5. A young wrestler in full gear wears a singlet, headgear, and wrestling shoes. Kneepads are optional.

EQUIPMENT

Wrestling requires very little equipment. Most youth programs require only sneakers and gym clothes for the young athletes just getting started. Clothes should have no zippers or other metal parts, which could injure a wrestler. Don't wear any jewelry or have anything in your pockets. Once you're sure that this is a sport worth pursuing, you could buy a pair of wrestling shoes, headgear, kneepads, and a singlet (Photo 5).

Shoes. A wrestling shoe should fit like a sock and lace all the way up to about ankle height. The shoe must be rubber-soled, with the upper portion constructed from leather, mesh, or polyester. Equipment varies in quality and price.

Headgear. A wrestler needs to protect the ears because they are one of the most common areas for injury. The headgear or ear guards have a Velcro or small buckle strapping system going over the top of the head, behind the head, and under the chin. These adjustable straps hold the cushioned ear cups in place. Headgear is not required for Olympic or international competition, but it is required for collegiate, high school, and younger competition. Some wrestlers also wear plastic mouthguards to protect their teeth.

Singlets. Singlets are very close-fitting nylon or spandex one-piece uniforms that must be worn by all wrestlers who enter tournaments and competitions. The singlet stretches from the shoulders to the thighs. Singlets are not usually worn during practice sessions; most wrestlers opt for T-shirts and shorts during workouts. Boys and men must wear underwear under singlets. Women are allowed to wear sports bras as well (no metal parts, however).

Kneepads. Worn to keep the knees from getting bruised, kneepads are optional. Typically they are tight-fitting, shock-absorbing cushions made of Lycra. Measure around the center of the knee for proper sizing.

Mat. All wrestling should be done on a cushioned mat. The mat is not more than 4" (10 cm) thick. It is made of foam covered with a thick, rubbery plastic. The mat has one large circle painted on it, which is 28' (8.6 m) in diameter for high school wrestling and 32' to 42' (9.8 to 13 m) in diameter for college wrestling. There is a smaller (10' or 3 m) circle marked its the center, which is the area in which wrestlers must start their competition. There is a 1' × 3' (30.5 × 91.5 cm) rectangle in the center of the smaller circle where the wrestlers always begin the match. There is a 5' (1.5 m) safety belt, or protection area, around the large circle. The area just inside the large circle is called the passivity zone; when the wrestlers reach this area, the referee might tell the wrestlers to move back inside.

GETTING PHYSICALLY AND MENTALLY FIT 2

A STRONG WORK ETHIC

To become a successful wrestler, you will have to work hard, watch your eating habits, and focus on muscle development. If you think it doesn't sound easy, you are right. It takes a lot of discipline and determination. Here's something to think about: Nothing worthwhile ever is easy.

What makes wrestling a worthwhile sport? Here are a few benefits to the sport. First, you will develop a mental edge through the use of different approaches and strategies, which carries over to having high self-esteem and self-confidence in other areas of your life. You will also, over time, develop in strength, flexibility, and in your overall ability to endure. You will figure out how your body functions and what works best for you.

Although wrestling is an individual sport, you are part of a team, with a coach and team guidelines to follow. This teaches you how to work and get along with others, how to be a leader, and how to follow rules and be a member of a group of people working toward the same goals. These are life skills that will take you places (Photo 1).

1. A strong work ethic on the mat often carries over to schoolwork and other areas of life.

Friendships formed through this sport can last a lifetime. As you learn and grow with your teammates, one of the biggest things you will face is how to deal with success and failure. Champions learn how to take the peaks and valleys in stride.

THE WONDERS OF WATER

A healthy, well-rounded diet and proper nutrition are very important for wrestlers of all ages. Keeping your body well hydrated with water and eating healthy foods will maintain stores of energy in your muscles. It is important to drink water before, during, and after workouts. The human body is 45% to 75% water by weight. Blood is almost 80% water. Water is involved in some way in every bodily process (Photo 2).

Your body uses water for cleaning purposes, flushing out toxins that are naturally produced by all bodies. By getting rid of these toxins, your internal systems run cleaner and your organs are

hydrated. Drinking water also lubricates your joints, keeps your skin healthy looking, and prevents it from drying out.

Did you know that your body has a built-in air-conditioning system? And guess what it needs to keep it running properly — water! Think about it. When your body gets hot, you sweat. As the sweat evaporates from your skin, your body cools off. If you don't drink water to replace what you lose when you sweat, your circulation becomes sluggish and your blood can become thick, which strains the heart.

It's important for an athlete to avoid dehydration. Dehydration occurs when your fluid losses are so great that your body can no longer sweat, and your body temperature can increase to a dangerous high. Even mild dehydration can cause headaches, dizziness, and an overall sick feeling.

The early warning signs of dehydration are thirst, fatigue, dizziness, headache, clumsiness, and nausea. You are in dangerous territory when you have muscle spasms, shriveled skin, painful urination, or feel delirious.

The best way to prevent dehydration is to drink 16 ounces (480 mL) of water about two hours

2. You lose a lot of water during a workout, so take time before, during, and after wrestling workouts to restore it.

TECHNIQUE, FUNDAMENTALS, AND DRILLING

TOM BRANDS

When 1996 Olympic gold medalist Tom Brands talks about wrestling, it is easy to see that the sport is his passion.

Wrestling has been a way of life for Tom and twin brother Terry for as long as they can remember. The earliest days of their wrestling looked more like rough-housing or tumbling. The Brands brothers started to learn the formal art of wrestling when they were in 5th grade in Sheldon, Iowa.

The brawl part of wrestling came very easy to Tom. The hardest aspect of wrestling for him was technique, but he stuck with the basics of the sport, which carried him to an Olympic gold medal in 1996.

As a wrestling coach at Iowa, Tom Brands preaches extreme discipline and a regimented lifestyle. He feels that wrestling is a good life-skills sport. "Wrestling, like many things in life, is all about accountability. You have to stand on your own two feet and make the right decisions for yourself. Most of all, don't make excuses for things," he said.

Tom Brands feels that strength training, conditioning, and technique are all equally important. Nutrition is a crucial facet, along with mental toughness.

"This is a sport where the best wrestler doesn't always win, but the most disciplined wrestler does. The athlete who is the most disciplined puts wrestling on a level that most opponents can't react to or understand," he said. "There is an intense inner satisfaction when you pin your opponent. It's the ultimate feeling in wrestling."

Tom Brands knows firsthand how much work it takes to succeed in wrestling. He had to work diligently on technique. He accomplished this through the discipline of drilling.

"Fundamentals are very important. When you are on your feet, you should be thinking: hit, drive, and finish. When you are on the mat, you are going for hand control. Make sure you keep your head up and butt down," he said.

"You have to work on your durability," he notes. "Don't neglect any one area. Go through the paces and you'll be a winner."

before a match or practice. About 15 minutes before exercising, drink another 8 ounces (240 mL) of water. During your workout, be sure to take the time to drink 6 ounces (180 mL) of fluids every 20 minutes to replace the lost fluids and to prevent overheating. Cold fluids are generally the best choice because they tend to cool your body faster.

After exercising, it is important to keep on drinking water to rehydrate. Any weight that is lost during a workout is generally water weight, so it is a good idea to replace those fluids.

Some athletes prefer sports drinks over water. Endurance athletes do need to replace the sodium and potassium, also known as the electrolytes, lost through sweat. Many sports drinks contain electrolytes, but if you are watching your weight, keep in mind that sports drinks are high in calories.

If water seems boring to drink, try varying the beverages you choose: fruit juice, flavored seltzer water, sports drinks, or decaffeinated beverages. Avoid caffeine, because caffeinated drinks (including cola drinks) make you urinate more, which works against you if you are focusing on rehydrating.

NUTRITION AND WEIGHT

Because they are involved in school, sports, and other activities, young athletes often have busy schedules and sometimes skip meals. Try to make nutrition a priority. Variety is important in a well-balanced diet. There is no one perfect food that can give your body all of the 50 nutrients it needs for top performance. Tell yourself before each day: If I eat well, I will wrestle well. There is no reason to miss a meal.

Your body requires carbohydrates for energy, protein to build and repair muscles, and calories to support the exercise needed to stimulate muscle growth. It also needs other basic nutrients. If you deprive your body in any of these areas, you won't have strong muscles, which could affect your overall ability to reach your potential. Wrestlers burn a lot more energy than people who aren't wrestling, so — not surprisingly — they have to eat more, but a well-balanced diet is the way to go.

Make sure your diet includes iron and calcium. Iron helps form the red blood cells that carry oxygen throughout your body. Calcium is important to help make your bones strong enough to withstand exercise, among other things. You can usually fulfill your calcium requirements with just three milk products a day. There are other calcium-rich foods such as tofu, spinach, kale, broccoli, and beans, as well as fortified foods like orange juice and apple juice, which can help with meeting your calcium needs.

Try to keep your intake of junk food to a minimum. Junk food gives you calories and a lot of fat. Try to train yourself to eat well-balanced meals and snack on fruit or vegetables in between meals so that the temptation to load up on junk food will be kept under control (Photo 3).

3. Taking time out for a healthy snack is a smart move for wrestlers of all ages.

Wrestling is a sport that matches athletes by their body weights for competition and workout purposes. As you gain skill and move toward competition, you will become aware of what your weight class is. That is a good time to visit a doctor and talk about your ideal weight and what percent body fat is healthy for you. It is also a good time to discuss nutrition with your doctor and get a nutrition plan if you are overweight.

In the past, wrestlers sometimes made themselves very sick or even died by trying to lose weight fast to stay in their weight class. Beware of quick weight-loss fads and techniques. These don't work and can be dangerous. Quick weight-loss schemes also can lead to loss of muscle mass and strength.

STRETCHING

A good conditioning program should start with a light jog and some basic stretching, done at a comfortable level. There should not be any discomfort in your workout if you stretch to loosen your muscles and get the blood flowing to them before exercising. Stretching helps to improve flexibility, which can prevent injuries, stiffness, and any discomfort you may feel from vigorous exercise. Below are some basic exercises.

4. Stretching the hamstrings increases flexibility.

Hamstring Stretch. Hamstrings are the tendons that attach to the leg muscles in the back of your knee. Sitting on the floor with your feet spread apart, reach with your hands to hold your feet. Do not bounce. Hold this stretch for 20 seconds, rest, and then repeat it (Photo 4).

Quadriceps Stretch. The quadriceps is a muscle in the front of the thigh. Stand next to a wall or another person (if you need to for balance), use one hand to help balance while you hold your ankle with your other hand, and gently pull your heel toward your back. Once you feel a good stretch, hold it for 20 seconds. Switch to the other leg and repeat the stretch (Photo 5).

Groin Stretch. The groin is the side part of the abdomen, just above the crease where your thighs attach to your body. Sitting down, bend your knees outward and bring the bottoms of both feet together. Gently press your knees to the ground; hold for 30 seconds. Repeat several times.

5. The quadriceps stretch warms up the muscles in the front of the thigh.

Calf Stretch. Your calf is the lower back portion of your leg below the knee. Facing a wall, lean forward with both hands pressing into the wall if you need a wall for balance. Otherwise put hands on one knee, as shown. Put one foot in front of the other about your shoulders-width apart. As you lean into this stretch, press the heel of your back foot toward the ground. Hold this for 30 seconds, and switch feet (Photo 6).

Arm Circles. A good way to warm up your arms and shoulders is to hold your arms straight out to the sides and circle in a forward motion for 50 repetitions (reps). Then stop and circle backward for 50 reps.

Push-ups. Push-ups get your upper body warmed up and are good for conditioning, too. Start on your stomach with your legs slightly apart. Place your hands palm down on the floor under your shoulders. Push your body up off the ground while your toes stay touching the ground for support. Keeping your back straight, push your body up and down, but don't touch the ground when you come down. Repeat as many times as you can (Photos 7 and 8).

6. This stretch warms up the calf muscles in the back of your lower leg.

7, 8. Push-ups are great for conditioning the arm muscles.

Sit-ups. Sit-ups help to keep your stomach muscles toned. Start on your back with your knees bent and legs slightly apart, with your feet flat on the ground. Criss-cross your arms in front of you, with your hands touching your shoulders. Bring your upper body up off the ground about one-third of the way toward your knees (Photo 9). You can also do sit-ups with your hands touching behind your head and your elbows held straight out to the sides (Photo 10). If you choose to do them this way, make sure you keep your chin upward and don't pull on your neck.

Pull-ups. If you have a pull-up bar available, reach up and grip it with your palms facing you. Pull your body up until your chin is even with the bar. If you are just beginning, get some help with this motion. Come down slowly before you pull yourself back up.

Skipping Rope and Running. Light running and skipping rope will get your muscles warmed up pretty quickly too, and are good before and after a workout.

9, 10. Sit-ups strengthen the abdominal muscles.

The photos below show you the location of some body parts, muscles, and tendons we refer to in the book.

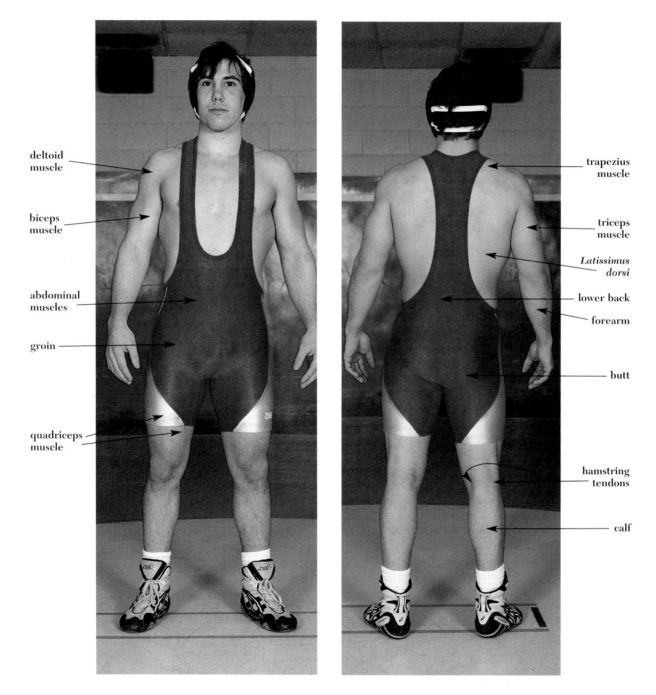

deltoid muscle

biceps muscle

abdominal muscles

groin

quadriceps muscle

trapezius muscle

triceps muscle

Latissimus dorsi

lower back

forearm

butt

hamstring tendons

calf

WRESTLING PRACTICE

Here's what you can expect at a typical practice.

Elementary Level

Wrestling season generally starts at the end of November and lasts until the beginning of March. Practice time for elementary school wrestlers is usually twice a week for one hour.

During a practice session, the coach will warm up the wrestlers with some light running, stretching, sit-ups, and push-ups. Each practice session will focus on a review of moves already mastered, and one or two new fundamental moves are introduced. The coach will call all the wrestlers together and demonstrate a move on an assistant coach. After he shows the move step by step, the wrestlers then find a space on the mat with a partner who is close in size. The wrestlers practice the move on each other. The coach goes around to each group and watches carefully to make sure the move is being executed properly. In many wrestling clubs, high school wrestlers are there to help demonstrate moves or to supervise how moves are being done.

There are also many drills that a coach uses to keep the practice fun and interesting. The wrestlers should not be overworked in a practice, because it is kept basic and fun and there are plenty of water breaks.

Besides stretching, exercising, and drills, the coach also allows time for live wrestling. At this level, the coach will allow the wrestlers to try a practice match with three 1-minute periods. The focus here is on learning and having fun, not on winning or losing.

Junior High and High School

On the junior high and high school levels, practice time is generally on weekdays for two hours. There is also a much stronger emphasis on conditioning. Much of the conditioning is done through drill work.

The coach uses the time to go deeper into instruction. Instead of teaching one or two basic moves, he can now instruct the wrestlers in more detail and for series of moves. When the coach allows for live wrestling in practice, it is usually for a full 6-minute match (Photo 13) for high school; for junior high school students, a match is 4½ minutes. Competition at this level takes place on a

13. Two wrestlers at practice.

regular basis throughout the week, as schools challenge each other in matches and tournaments.

STRENGTH TRAINING

All athletes should try to add the element of power to their wrestling. Strength is as important an element to success in wrestling as conditioning, technique, and nutrition (Photo 14).

14. Strength training pays off when it comes down to tough competition on the mat.

Cross Training

For young athletes, one of the best ways to gain strength is by playing other sports during the off-season, which is called cross training. Cross training gives growing muscles the chance to develop through a variety of exercise and will help to improve your coordination, quickness, and flexibility. Young athletes who have not yet completed puberty should not weight train, because lifting weights could harm their skeletal development. Instead, athletes as young as 3rd grade can do push-ups, pull-ups, sit-ups, and dips to increase strength. Running will build your stamina, which you will need to get through a 6-minute match. Start out slowly and increase

your distance as your endurance builds.

Provided a doctor gives the go-ahead, a 7th or 8th grader can begin supervised light weight training. Form and technique are crucial in weight training, so it is imperative to work with someone educated in fitness, such as a coach or physical education instructor.

Many wrestlers think that going to practice and competition alone will maintain their strength during the season. This is simply not true. Proper strength-training workouts, coordinated by your coach or fitness instructor, must include circuit training and more repetitions. Strength training

FOCUSING

TERRY BRANDS

Terry Brands won a bronze medal for the United States at the 2000 Olympics in Sydney, Australia. Here he summarizes his advice for everyone involved in the sport.

"The biggest thing is to stay focused on your tasks. Don't worry about the repetitive nature of wrestling. Look at your goals, and focus on getting better every time you step on the mat," Terry Brands says. He is currently a wrestling coach at the University of Nebraska.

He knows firsthand what it takes to be a champion. "It all boils down to drilling. It's hard. It's monotonous. It's what you have to do to be the best. The basics of wrestling are very important, even at the higher levels."

Terry Brands likes to cross-train as well. He has always done running, weight lifting — either heavy weights or circuits — biking, rope climbing, and hill workouts, in which he runs outdoors for a change in scenery.

during the season is important, as long as it is approved by your physician.

Basic Training Ideas

Intensity is the most important aspect of strength training. While you are training in-season, work hard and fast, because this helps endurance. In the off-season, a slower paced workout is advisable.

Consistency is the key to success. Missed workouts confuse your body and throw your training off course. Each athlete's body responds differently to workouts, so do not get discouraged. You will get there!

It is a good idea to train with similar movements to those used in wrestling and to use a full range of motion. Power cleans and pummel curls are good examples for the more mature and advanced wrestler.

Weight Training

The purpose of weight training is to strengthen the muscles, increase muscular endurance, and prevent or heal injuries. All schools and fitness centers use weight systems. Use what is available to you: universal, free weights, dumbbells, nautilus, treadmills, Air-o-dyne, and rowing machines all are useful. If nothing else is available, run stairs, jump rope, climb ropes, use trees and rocks. Don't make excuses, just make it happen.

Make sure you space your workouts. Early-morning weight training is best, because you need at least five hours' recuperation time before wrestling practice. Also, never weight train in the same muscle group two days in a row, because your muscles need to recover from intense workouts.

When you plan your personal fitness program with your coach, make sure you have a well-rounded plan and stick to it. All of the major muscle groups — chest, back, arms, shoulders, and legs — must be worked. Your neck, stomach, and forearms also are important. It's also good to have a buddy system in which you have a workout partner so you can encourage and help each other.

3 THE BASIC RULES

A LITTLE HISTORY

Wrestling is one of the oldest competitive sports known to humans. Wrestling became an Olympic sport at the 18th Olympiad in 708 BC in Greece. Many other ancient civilizations left clues that wrestling was a part of their culture, including the Egyptians, Japanese, Chinese, Turks, and peoples of the British Isles. There are drawn images of wrestlers on the walls in the temple tombs of Beni Hasan near the Nile River in Egypt portraying hold and takedown combinations dating back to 2000 BC. Interestingly, these moves are still prevalent in all levels of wrestling today. Caves in France have drawings from 20,000 years ago illustrating wrestlers in competition.

Greek mythology tells of mighty Greek gods wrestling for possession of the Earth on mountain peaks. The Bible recounts disputes that were settled by wrestling matches. Mythic stories tell of an ancient Sumerian ruler named Gilgamesh who used his strength to save the city of Uruk.

For centuries there were many local and regional folkstyles of wrestling. Early in the 19th century, the modern style of Greco-Roman wrestling was developed. Greco-Roman was the only form of wrestling in the modern Olympic Games until 1904, when freestyle was added.

The international governing body that sets standards for wrestling is FILA (*Fédération Internationale des Luttes Associées*), founded in 1912. FILA gave wrestling rules, standards, and organized competitions. Each country has its own national governing body (NGB) as well, within the FILA framework. For the United States the NGB is USA Wrestling. In the UK it's the British Amateur Wrestling Association. In Canada the NGB is the Canadian Amateur Wrestling Association. The NGB is a good source of information about rules and competitions.

WRESTLING STYLES

There are three basic styles of wrestling: folkstyle, freestyle, and Greco-Roman.

Folkstyle, also called collegiate or scholastic wrestling, is the style used in the United States from elementary school age right up through junior high, high school, and college. Holds below the waist and leg holds are allowed. In folkstyle wrestling you can't throw an opponent directly backward from a back-arch, which is allowed in freestyle. Your opponent must be turned to the side to avoid a slam penalty.

Freestyle is derived from the upright wrestling of the Greeks and Lancashire no-holds-barred regional style. It is very similar to folkstyle. It is used internationally in most parts of the world, and also in the Olympics. Girls and women in the US usually compete freestyle. Internationally, women wrestlers compete freestyle.

Greco-Roman is another form of wrestling used in the Olympics. In Greco-Roman, you are not allowed to use your legs in holds or to attack you opponent's legs, nor are any holds below the waist allowed.

THE MATCH

Here's a brief summary of how a high school folkstyle match progresses. There are 3 periods of 2 minutes each. The time and some details vary for junior high school and college levels. Usually several officials are involved: a referee, who runs the bout on the mat and makes decisions on points; a judge, who keeps score; and a mat chairman, who decides a score if the referee and judge disagree. Hand signals, words, and whistles are used by the referee to communicate with the judge.

First Period

▌▌▌ Two opponents come onto the mat and take their stances in the neutral position (Photo 1).

1. Two wrestlers in the neutral position on the starting lines.

▌▌▌ The two wrestlers shake hands and the referee blows his whistle to start the action.
▌▌▌ The wrestlers engage in hand fighting as they try to create angles on each other.
▌▌▌ One wrestler decides to make the first move. If he executes a takedown, the referee awards him two points. From there he tries to turn his oppo-

nent to his back to either pin him or get "back points" for holding him on his back.

▌▌▌ If the wrestler on the bottom who was taken down can get out and escape from his opponent, the referee will award him one point for an escape.

▌▌▌ The referee blows the whistle when 2 minutes are up, and all action stops where it is.

Second Period

▌▌▌ Based on a coin toss, one wrestler is allowed to choose if he wants to start on the top, bottom, neutral position — or he can defer the choice to the other wrestler.

▌▌▌ The wrestlers are down on the mat in the referee's position (Photo 2). The referee blows the whistle to start the action. The top wrestler tries to break down his opponent (flatten his opponent on the mat); the bottom wrestler tries to escape.

2. The referee's position. Note hands on starting line.

▌▌▌ If at any point the wrestlers go out of bounds, they must come back to the center of the mat and start in the referee's position again.

▌▌▌ The referee signals the scorer's table whenever a wrestler scores.

▌▌▌ The period ends after two minutes have elapsed.

Third Period

▌▌▌ The third period starts with the second wrestler choosing if he wants to start in the top, bottom, or neutral position.

▌▌▌ The action starts when the referee blows the whistle, and he signals the scorer's table when a wrestler is awarded points.

▌▌▌ The period is over at the end of two minutes.

▌▌▌ Both wrestlers go to the center circle and shake hands, and the referee raises the arm of the winner.

SCORING POINTS

The main objective in wrestling is to either pin your opponent or to score more points than your opponent. A pin occurs when an opponent's back is pressed to the mat and both shoulders are held down. For a pin to occur at the high school or younger levels in folkstyle wrestling, the wrestler must hold his opponent's shoulders against the mat for 2 seconds. In freestyle wrestling and Greco-Roman wrestling, the shoulders are held down for one second for a pin.

At a match, the referee wears a red wristband and a green wristband, one on each wrist. Green

3. The top wrestler has excellent control of the bottom wrestler in blue and is very close to pinning his shoulders to the mat.

represents the home team player and red represents the visitor in matches with 2 teams. Each wrestler is given either a red or green ankle band to make the scoring simpler. If the wrestler wearing the green band scores, the referee holds up his hand with the green wristband to signal the scorekeeper how many points to award the wrestler.

A referee gets a close look at the action during a college match.

A high school match consists of three periods that last 2 minutes each. A junior high school match has three periods of 1½ periods each. If there is no pin during the match, the wrestler with the most points wins. There are four basic ways to score points:

||| A takedown is worth two points. It occurs when you take your opponent down to the mat from a standing neutral position to gain control. When you have control, you are in the top or dominant position.

||| An escape is worth one point. An escape occurs when you get out of your opponent's control from the bottom position and end up standing in a neutral position.

||| A reversal is worth two points. It occurs when you escape from the bottom position and take control from your opponent. In one move you basically go from being the wrestler who was controlled to being the one now in control.

||| A nearfall is worth either two or three points. A nearfall occurs when a wrestler is close to getting pinned (Photo 3). If your opponent's shoulders are within 4" (10 cm) of the mat, at an angle of 45 degrees or less, for 2 to 4 seconds, you are awarded two points. A nearfall is worth three points if you hold your opponent's shoulders within 4" of the mat for 5 seconds or more.

ILLEGAL HOLDS, WARNINGS & PENALTIES

In amateur wrestling, you can lose points for injuring your opponent. Some holds are illegal because injury can easily occur when they are used. Wrestlers are warned once for using an illegal hold. Here are some examples:

||| A "chicken wing" and arm bar, which go against the opponent's joints, are illegal holds.

||| Clasping your hands is also an illegal hold if you are in the top position, because it is too easy to ride your opponent and waste time in a match. Clasping occurs when a wrestler in the top position connects his hands while any of his opponent's supporting body parts are down on the mat (Photo 4).

4. Clasping is illegal here, because the wrestler in blue has his knees down on the mat.

▓ A full nelson is also illegal because it is dangerous. A full nelson occurs when the top wrestler has both arms underneath his opponent's arms and he can touch his fingers behind his opponent's head (Photo 5).

5. The full nelson is an illegal hold.

You can also be warned for stalling. Stalling occurs when you delay the match by going out of bounds intentionally or by getting a passivity warning for not putting enough physical effort into wrestling, which delays the action. If a wrestler gets two warnings, he is penalized one point. If the wrestler continues to stall, he is penalized another point. A wrestler is disqualified if he receives two penalty points for stalling.

When the match is over, you must shake hands with your opponent and wait for the official decision declaring the winner. After the referee raises the hand of the winner, it is customary to shake the hand of the opponent's coach.

GIRLS AND WOMEN IN WRESTLING

Women wrestled in ancient Sparta, but in recent times women didn't get a chance to wrestle until the 20th century. Wrestling was traditionally considered a sport for boys and men.

The United States Girls Wrestling Association, established in 1998, reports that the number of girls wrestling has increased each year. Its national championship had 272 girls in 1998 and more than 500 wrestlers in 2001. A survey conducted by the National High School Federation reported that over 2500 girls in the US were on high school wrestling teams in the year 2000. In the US, it is becoming more common to see girls on high school wrestling teams. Some states, such as Michigan, have all-girls high school state wrestling tournaments. Since 1990, there has been a Women's National Tournament in the U.S., sponsored by USA Wrestling.

In the US women usually wrestle freestyle, and they wrestle freestyle internationally as well. When a girl gets involved in the sport, it is likely that she will be the only female in the wrestling room and that she will have to compete against men. As the number of females in wrestling increases, more female wrestling clubs and teams will emerge in the US. This is already true in Canada, where there is female wrestling at all age levels, and there are high school and college women's wrestling teams.

NOTES FROM A WOMAN WRESTLER

VICKIE ZUMMO

Vickie Zummo, 23 in 2001, has been wrestling since she was in 6th grade. When she won a county championship in middle school and proved just how good she really was, she made a difficult decision to move away from her family to train with a top coach in freestyle wrestling.

Zummo is a three-time US Nationals Champion. During her first year competing at the Nationals, she was named Most Outstanding Wrestler. From there she competed in the World Team Trials Championship, where she won a bronze medal for the United States.

Becoming a member of the United States Women's World team took a great deal of preparation and dedication. "I gave up most of my life to train for this level of wrestling," Zummo notes. "The stamina that is needed is tremendous. I cross-train with weight workouts, mountain biking, running, and any way that I can move my body. I also like to train with men because they are so aggressive and they really push me. The greatest compliment comes at the end of a workout when the men say, 'Wow, you're tough.'"

She notes, "I never experienced males not wanting to wrestle me, but I have heard of some females having difficulties, because not everyone is open-minded. My advice to the girls who are getting into wrestling is to just keep your heads up. If you want it, then you should go for it. Gain it for yourself. Go to practice and work hard, because you will get good at it."

As this book goes to press, Zummo has her head up and she is focusing on the year 2004, when it is possible that women's wrestling will be an Olympic sport. "I am working hard and I am confident. Before every match I am thinking: 'Who trained harder to be here? Who has more heart?' And the answer is always: 'Me!'"

4 STARTING POSITIONS

Wrestling is a journey. Many elite athletes feel they could wrestle for 20 years and they would still just scratch the surface as far as having a complete understanding of the sport. All advanced wrestlers will agree, however, that the basics always win.

The more you learn about the sport, the greater your chances are of staying in a good position and not getting caught off balance. Although the sport is extremely physical, there is no kick-ing, punching, biting, choking or intentionally try-ing to harm your opponent.

STANCE

The standing position from which each wrestler starts his moves is called a stance. At the start of the first period, each wrestler is in his stance in the neutral position on the mat. In the neutral posi-tion, both wrestlers are on their feet, and neither is in control. They are not touching. Each wrestler must have one foot on the starting line of the rectangle in the center of the mat; the other foot is either even with or behind the lead foot (Photo 1). A good wrestler tries to create scoring opportunities and always has to be prepared to have an answer to an attack. Having a consistently good stance is the best line of defense.

2. The squared stance, front view.

1. The first period starts with each wrestler in his stance in the neutral position.

3. The squared stance, side view.

In the squared stance (Photos 2 and 3), your toes and knees are aligned and are the same distance apart as your shoulders. You are on the balls of the feet, your knees and elbows are slightly bent, and your elbows must be held tight into the body, making it harder to grab them. Shoulders should be slightly shrugged, with the neck bowed and eyes focused on the opponent's midsection.

The staggered stance, with one foot in front of the other, is a more offensive stance, because it puts a wrestler in position to shoot in (move in fast) on the opponent. It is important to be on the balls of the feet. The knees should be slightly bent, the head is up, back is straight, elbows are held close to the body, and both hands are held out in front (Photo 4). All wrestlers must learn to be steady on their feet to avoid losing balance and being brought down to the mat.

4. The staggered stance has one foot in front of the other, with the knees and elbows slightly bent.

REFEREE'S POSITION

A coin toss decides which wrestler gets to choose his position in the second period, whether on the top, in the bottom, or in the neutral position (standing apart from the opponent). The starting position in which one wrestler is on the top and one is on the bottom is called the referee's position. The referee's position also is used to restart the match after the wrestlers go out of bounds.

The third period starts with the second wrestler making his choice of the same three positions.

In the referee's position, the bottom wrestler kneels with knees as far apart as possible and both

5. In the referee's position, the bottom wrestler has a sturdy base with his head held up, and his weight drops toward his hips. The top wrestler, who can set up on either side of his opponent, cups his hand slightly above the other wrestler's closest elbow, leans onto the opponent's back with his chest, and reaches his free arm around the waist with the palm pressing into the navel area.

ankles flat to the mat so they can't be grabbed easily (Photo 5). His toes should be together so that a triangle is formed from the knees to the toes. The bottom wrestler's palms are flat on the mat at least 12 inches (30.5 cm) in front of his knees, and his head is held up.

The top wrestler can position himself on either side of the opponent. With one hand cupped like a "C", he grips the opponent slightly above the closest elbow. He leans onto the opponent's back with his chest and reaches his free arm around his opponent's waist, with his palm pressing into the navel area. The referee will examine the starting position and then blow the whistle to begin the wrestling.

Bottom Position

The bottom wrestler has the weight of the top wrestler on him. For this reason it is good to get out of the bottom position as soon as possible. The key to success in the bottom position is to utilize leg, hip, and thigh strength to stand up and escape from the opponent. It is important to be explosive from the bottom. The goal is to escape or get a reversal.

Start with a good base position and keep the hips underneath the rest of the body, because the opponent is trying to control the hips (Photo 6). The hips are a wrestler's center of gravity, where most of his weight is concentrated. Next, bring up the inside leg (the leg closest to the opponent). Keep the back straight, fight for hand control, sit out (sit back) by scooting the hips outward, stand

6. The bottom wrestler tries to maintain a good position during a match.

up, turn in, and step away. Release the opponent's hands when it feels safe. The referee will score one point for an escape for the wrestler who breaks free from the bottom to a neutral position.

Photos 7 through 9 show a young wrestler escaping from the bottom position.

Top Position

The wrestler in the top position does not want to give up control. The goal from the top is to break down the opponent and turn him onto his back (Photo 10). If the bottom wrestler is held down in the back position with his shoulders at an angle of 45 degrees or less, within 4" (10 cm) of the mat for 2 seconds, the top wrestler gains two points. When a wrestler's shoulders are exposed to the mat this way it is called a nearfall. If the hold lasts for 5 seconds, three points are awarded, which is the maximum for back points. If the top wrestler holds the opponent's shoulder blades to the mat for 2 seconds, the opponent is pinned and the match is over.

10. The top wrestler (red) has a good head position because he can use it to drive the bottom wrestler toward the mat.

7, 8, 9. The bottom wrestler tries to escape as he gets up to his knees, brings his leg out, and drives upward to a standing position.

HEAD POSITION

Head position is key because it opens up offensive opportunities and it can also be the first line of defense. If a wrestler's head is in position, the opponent should never have an opportunity to attack. When a wrestler is moving, his body tends to follow his head. The best position for the head is upward, because it allows for clear vision and a better opportunity to see the opponent's next move and create your own scoring positions.

As the two wrestlers are on their feet, head to head (Photo 11), they are hand fighting and trying to attack each other from the side with quick motions. A good wrestler is constantly in motion, creating angles on the opponent and trying to knock the opponent off balance. No matter what tie-up is used in an attack, it is important to maintain a good head position to keep the rest of the body aligned.

TIE-UPS

The lock or hold that a wrestler in the neutral position uses to control his opponent and lead to a takedown is called a tie-up. A takedown is any move in which one opponent takes another from his feet to the mat, where the wrestler who started the takedown ends up in the top position, scoring 2 points. Here are three frequently used tie-ups. More tie-ups are discussed in the chapter on hand fighting.

11. As the wrestlers spar for inside hand control, they are positioned head to head in a staggered stance.

1. Collar tie-up with inside arm control: Clamp one hand behind your opponent's neck. Place your forearm in the center of his chest. With your other hand, grasp the inside of his arm just above the elbow (Photo 12).

2. Collar-wrist tie-up: Clamp one hand behind your opponent's neck and use the other hand to grasp his wrist.

3. Double-wrist tie-up: Here you gain control of your opponent by getting a firm grip on both of his wrists (Photo 13).

12. Red demonstrates a collar tie-up with inside arm control.

13. Blue controls his opponent by tying up both his wrists in a double-wrist tie-up.

WINNING AND LOSING

TOM BRANDS

Tom Brands was a 1996 Olympic gold medalist in wrestling. For Tom and his twin brother Terry, wrestling has always been a way of life. The brawling part of wrestling came easily to Tom. Tom Brands likes to force his brawling style on an opponent. "I get on his head, pass elbows, and get on his wrists. When I lay my hands on him, I keep my feet moving. My theory is to have heavy hands and light feet. By doing this, he feels my weight and I can move him," Tom said, adding: "Try to take your wrestling to a higher level. There's nothing to be afraid of. It's not life or death. Just go out there and perform on the mat and let it happen."

Tom Brands knows that smart, hard-nosed, aggressive wrestling will bring success. When Tom Brands was at Iowa State he won three national titles in 1990, 1991, and 1992 at 134 pounds. He was also a state champion when he was in high school.

One of the most difficult things is handling a loss, especially if it is a big loss. "Everybody's been beaten at some time. How a person gets over that loss is key. You have to get yourself to the top no matter what it takes, but if you don't get there, then it's very important to move on. The reality check here is that not everybody wins," he notes.

HAND FIGHTING AND CREATING ANGLES 5

hile you are in the neutral position, your main goal is to unbalance your opponent. Through pushing, pulling, faking shots, and staying in constant motion, you will create scoring opportunities. Your hands are heavy on your opponent, while you remain light on your feet. Your ability to create angles and put yourself in scoring positions will determine your success on your feet. By attacking your opponent's left side, right side, and head in sequence, you will keep him off balance, resulting in many scoring opportunities.

In order to set up an attack, use your skills in hand fighting and creating angles. Head position is very important also (Photo 1 and 2). Because they are such an important facet of having success on your feet, you should drill these skills often.

The best time to drill hand fighting is when you are very tired during a practice session. The chance of getting injured in hand fighting is minimal. The objective in a hand fighting drill is to create angles on your opponent, recognize that you have done so, but not move in and attack the opponent. You are in essence just concentrating on the unbalancing part of the attack.

1 and 2. Two opponents head to head. Head position is crucial when you are on your feet.

UNBALANCING THE OPPONENT: CREATING ANGLES AND MOTION

Forward Motion Setup — Steering-Wheel Motion

This move is done by placing a hand on the back of the opponent's head just above the neck and pulling it forward and slightly downward in a circular motion (Photo 3). At the same time, you must change your location by stepping either backward or backward in a circular motion to either side of your hand that has the tie-up. This movement puts your opponent in a weak position, because he either has to go with your movements or he has to resist them, which throws off his balance.

As you use the steering-wheel motion, your foot position should be in the penetration-step stance and your feet should be shoulders-width apart. Step with your foot to the back of his heel on the same side as his tie-up hand. From here, there could be an opportunity for a single- or double-leg takedown.

3. Red demonstrates a steering-wheel motion. His right hand is positioned on the back of his opponent's neck, his left hand is on the triceps, and he pulls both forward and downward in a circular motion.

Backward Motion Setup

Another way to throw your opponent off balance is by forcing him into a circular motion, moving to the left and right as you attack. You can put your opponent in this motion by tapping him on the chest or shoulder while moving toward him, by circling into your tie-ups, or by pushing his head backward with your hand.

Side Motion Setup

While you are trying to set up with forward and backward movements, a quick side motion to the left or the right will force your opponent to react. As he is reacting, you should either try for a takedown or make another move. Passing elbows is another way of creating a side motion (Photo 4).

Downward Motion Setup

One of the more popular setups at all levels uses a downward motion. The downward motion is done with a head tie-up as you move forward into your opponent and pull him down. Your opponent's reaction is usually to pull away, which will create a new chance to attack.

Arm Drag

You can move your opponent and control his hips with the arm drag. With this move, begin by grabbing hold of his wrist and pulling his arm diagonally across his chest. Focusing on the controlled arm, secure your free hand above his elbow (Photo 5), and pull down hard toward the mat. Position your body so that you are now shoulder to shoulder and toe to toe. As you are pulling your opponent's arm toward the mat, lower your hips and reach for his far hip.

5. Blue doubled up on his opponent's left wrist, and then moved his hand up to red's triceps muscle for an arm drag.

4. Wrestlers can also move each other by passing elbows. The wrestler in blue controls his opponent's right elbow by pulling it down and across his own body, while using his right hand to attack a leg.

CONTROLLING POSITIONS

Inside Tie-up and Outside Tie-up

The inside tie-up is a hand-fighting position that helps you to move your opponent when you are in the standing position. This tie-up can be set up to either side of your opponent. Your inside tie can be high and wrapped around the back of the armpit. Your hand can be cupped or your thumb can be in the armpit but underneath the shoulder, your elbows should be down, and your head should be on the same side as the inside tie.

If you have an inside tie, your opponent will have an outside tie (Photo 6). His four fingers will be toward the inside of your triceps, with his thumb on the outside. His elbow should be down as well.

Underhook

An underhook is another controlling position used to move your opponent (Photo 7). There are two basic ways you can gain an underhook. The

GETTING THROUGH TOURNAMENTS

TOM BRANDS

Once you have confidence and the green light from a coach to go ahead and test your skills in competition, there are many USA Wrestling sanctioned events held in local gymnasiums to attend, or similar competitions if you live in another country. (USA Wrestling is the national governing body, or NGB, for wrestling in the US. Each country has its own NGB.) Wrestling tournaments are very long and time-consuming. The time span between your personal matches varies, but there is traditionally a bit of a wait.

If you want to do well in a tournament, the most important thing you must avoid is getting "gym head" — that dull, drowsy feeling from being in a hot gym for long periods of time.

Olympic gold medalist Tom Brands knows how to avoid going stale in a tournament. He suggests getting out of the gym — but let your coach know what you're doing first. "The best bet is to get out and away. After your first match is over, untie your laces, go take a shower if there's time, and lie down somewhere. Focus on your own preparation. Keep light fluids and food going through your body. Take sips of water and eat small pieces of banana," Brands suggests.

Tom Brands notes that the last thing a wrestler wants to do is sit in the bleachers and watch more matches. Expending energy cheering for teammates or getting caught up in the emotions of another match is not wise. The other thing you don't want to do is sit around stewing about your next opponent. Instead, focus on what you need to do to get prepared for that next match.

"Wrestling is not a rah-rah sport. Don't get wrapped up in all the other matches if you're not done wrestling yet. Wrestling is very much an individual sport. The team wins because of individual wrestling efforts. The team needs individuals to rise to the occasion. Your teammates are counting on you to get the job done."

6. The wrestler on the right has an inside tie; the wrestler on the left has an outside tie.

7. Blue has an underhook on his opponent. Blue's left hand reaches under red's armpit and stops on the shoulder blade. The elbows are down.

first way is to snap or pull your opponent's head downward with the opposite hand from the one you're going to use for the underhook. If you're going to underhook with your left hand, you will snap with your right hand. You must keep your own head in position, regardless of what you are doing with your hands. If you snap with your right hand, take your left arm and place it under the right armpit of your opponent. Don't put your left arm in too deep, but just deep enough to get on to his lat (*Latissimus dorsi* muscle). Your elbows

should be down and your head in position.

The second way to get an underhook is from the inside tie and wrist tie-up. In each situation, be sure to keep your hips under you. Another way to gain an underhook is off a leg attack. After penetrating for a shot, immediately bring your left or right arm underneath your opponent's armpit, securing the underhook.

Two-on-One

When you shift both hands onto one of your opponent's arms, it is called a two-on-one (Photo 8). A two-on-one is a dominating tie up that will allow you to control your opponent and create many scoring opportunities, keeping your opponent on the defensive. To obtain a two-on-one on your opponent's left arm, you start by controlling his left wrist with your right hand. Next, take your left hand off your inside tie and double up on his wrist, and then crawl up his arm until your right hand is on his triceps muscle.

Another chance to get a two-on-one is when your opponent has his left hand on your head. Look away with your head while at the same time you catch his wrist with your right hand. Pull his arm in front of you and grab his triceps with your left hand.

8. Red moves his right hand up to the biceps of blue's left arm, and red's shoulder is on top of blue's shoulder. Red pulls blue's hand downward towards his foot.

Drills

Regardless of what level wrestler you are, there are some important fundamentals that you should drill during each workout. It is best to begin each workout by drilling all of these areas to ensure that they are covered thoroughly. Photos 9 through 11 show three effective ways of creating angles when hand fighting. Other important drills are: driving across opponent in a high-crotch or single-leg attack, defending a front headlock, and defending your opponent's attack with your head. These will be covered later in the book.

11. Blue controls red's elbow by passing it across in front of him and downward.

9. The wrestlers are hand fighting. Blue creates the angle — he grabs his opponent's triceps, pulling it down and across his body as he steps to the side.

10. Blue underhooks red's arm and lifts it to create an angle.

DEFENDING UNDERHOOKS AND TWO-ON-ONES

Let's take a look at how to get out of two-on-ones and underhooks. First, you always want to maintain your correct stance.

If your opponent has an underhook underneath your right arm, straighten your arm over his shoulder and circle to the left. The wrestler with an underhook wants to lift that side, so all of your weight must be down on that side. Do not allow him to lift that side as you circle. A common mistake is that wrestlers circle and do not keep pressure down on that side, which makes it easy for an opponent to lift the underhook and shoot. If the underhook is on your right arm, straighten your right arm and slip it through the little hole that you'll be creating by circling to your left.

When you are getting out of a two-on-one, always attack the top hand. If your opponent has a two-on-one on your right arm, you will attack the hand that is on the biceps. Another way is to attack your opponent's far elbow. If your opponent has a two-on-one on your right arm, you will attack his right elbow, pull it in toward you, but always maintain your head position.

FRONT HEADLOCK

A front headlock is a move that controls the upper body of your opponent, which creates many options offensively for you. When you catch your opponent in a front headlock, his chances of making any offensive moves are slim. The main objective of a front headlock is to get a good angle to attack your opponent's side. If you are over your opponent's head with your right arm, your elbow has to be down and your hand should not be past your opponent's collarbone on the side where you are over his head. Your opponent's head is underneath you. Your right shoulder is driving into your opponent's right trapezius muscle, and your right hand is on the neck near the throat (Photo 12).

Your left hand is on his right triceps and you pull the triceps toward you in a downward motion as you bring the hand that is over his neck down. You are basically trying to pinch his triceps and his head together (Photo 13), and as you do that you are going to circle to the left while pulling down and forward with a steady, constant pressure to create an angle. You are trying to create an angle by getting around to your left side or your opponent's right side.

A good drill is to have one wrestler getting into a front headlock and the other trying to get out.

12. Red is applying a front headlock. His right shoulder is driving into blue's right trapezius muscle, and red's right arm reaches over so that his hand is on the neck near blue's throat.

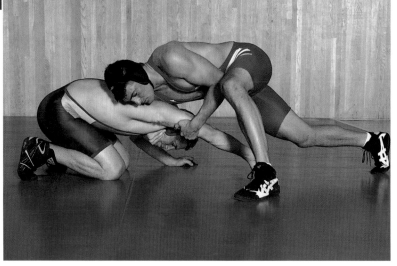

13. Red has his opponent in a front headlock. While the right hand hooks over blue's neck, red's left hand has a firm grip on his opponent's right triceps. Red pulls the right arm forward and to the right so that the head and triceps are pinched together.

Defending against the Front Headlock

If you are caught in a front headlock, you can't allow your opponent to get around to your side, because it will give him an angle, opening you up to a number of different attacks. You have to keep him in front of you. Take the elbow of his arm that is over your head and pull it toward you as you turn your head to the inside to loosen his hold, and drive across your opponent (Photos 14 and 15). This will prevent your opponent from getting around to your side. Throughout this move, you must put as much or more pressure onto your opponent as he puts onto you. If he has more pressure driving into you, then you're likely to get into some trouble.

Another way to defend against a front headlock is to pull the opponent's right triceps, which is over your head, toward you, rotate your hips in, and shoot to a high-crotch or duckunder.

As you seek to control your opponent, remember that the objective is to score, whether an opponent attacks you or you attack an opponent.

14, 15. Red is caught in a front headlock. As he drives his weight toward his opponent, red reaches up and pulls the elbow outward to release pressure on his neck and loosen the grip. He can now turn his head inside and drive across his opponent or get under his opponent's arm and attack his legs.

INSIDE PENETRATION STEP SERIES AND TAKEDOWNS

6

Earning the first takedown from the neutral position in the opening seconds of the first period of a match is crucial. There is a psychological bonus to scoring first that can give a wrestler an advantage throughout the match. From the initial sound of the referee's whistle, your strategy should be to dominate your opponent. Your hand-fighting skills, ability to create angles and move your opponent, combined with a powerful penetration step will bring you great success on your feet.

You earn two points for a takedown when you take your opponent to the mat and gain top control. Gaining control means that you are in the dominant position on top of your opponent, giving you an advantage.

It's interesting that some of the best wrestlers favor only two or three takedown moves that are consistent point-winners for them. As with all aspects of wrestling, the best advice is practice, practice, and more practice until you can do these moves with speed and efficiency. Constant drilling of the fundamental takedowns creates a quickness that is tough to counter.

LEVEL CHANGES

When it is time to set up, execute, counter, and finish moves, the initial motion begins with a level change. A level change is a basic and important skill. When executing a level change, the hips are lowered, bringing the chest down to the thigh. It is important to always remain in your stance, with good alignment of the knees and your feet at shoulders-width apart. Before shooting or moving in quickly on your opponent, make sure the opponent is within touching distance. Scoring opportunities are created by quick changes in level (Photos 1 and 2).

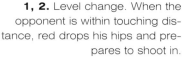

1, 2. Level change. When the opponent is within touching distance, red drops his hips and prepares to shoot in.

PENETRATION STEP

Once an attack is initiated on the legs or hips, the next move is to take a deep inside penetration step to go through an opponent's defenses. When the offensive wrestler drops his hips and shoots, he must remain in his stance as the lead shoulder drives into the opponent's stomach area. The opponent will either back up or sprawl as you drive across his body. Bring up your back leg to finish so your hips remain underneath you, allowing you to stay in a powerful and solid position (Photos 3 to 6).

3 to 6. Practicing the penetration step. From a stance position, change levels so that you are bending at the hips and lowering your chest to your thighs. Next, take a deep step forward with the lead or front foot in a heel to toe to knee motion, while the back leg drives forward and quickly drags forward to finish in base position with good alignment. Your arms hook around the opponent's legs.

DOUBLE-LEG TAKEDOWN

Once a good penetration step is established, perhaps the easiest move to learn is the double-leg takedown, in which you try to attack both legs and control your opponent's hips. This move begins with an aggressive inside penetration step; your lead foot steps inside the opponent's legs as deep as his feet are. As you shoot in low, your shoulders should be over your lead knee. Continue your penetration by driving into your opponent, drive down to the knee of your lead leg (Photo 7), and bring your other foot to the outside of his foot.

Once you shoot in from a low position, grasp your opponent tightly around the back of the legs or butt (Photo 8). Your head should be by his bottom rib on the side of your trail leg. Keep your shoulder positioned into his stomach. Bring your elbows tight against your hip bones. Lower your hips and drive across him; then lift him so his feet come off the ground and drive him backwards onto the mat (Photo 9).

7, 8, and 9. A double-leg takedown.

Arm Drag to a Double-Leg Takedown

The arm drag to a double-leg takedown is an additional double-leg takedown move, demonstrated in Photos 10, 11, and 12.

10. Red uses his right hand to reach to blue's triceps, and he pulls the arm down and across blue's body while stepping back and to the left.

11. With his weight transferred to his left leg, red penetrates between his opponent's feet with a big step with his right foot. Red changes his level and drives his shoulder into his opponent's hips.

12. Red continues to drive by pushing across with his neck and pinching his opponent's knees together with his hands.

Underhook to a Double-Leg Takedown

In Photos 13 through 17, red starts with an underhook and executes a double-leg takedown.

13. Red positions his head on the side opposite the one where he has an underhook.

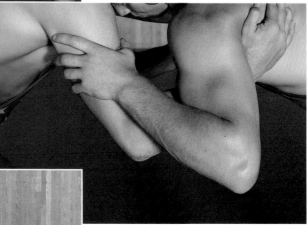

14. When blue posts, or touches on his shoulder with an extended arm, red pulls the underhook in tight to his body.

15. Red posts blue's right arm with red's palm facing away from him. Red moves his head away from blue about 6" (15 cm), creating space to get underneath blue's right elbow.

16. Red moves to throw his opponent over his shoulder while he settles his hips underneath blue.

17. Red quickly drops his hands behind blue's knees. Once red has his shoulder in tight, he will drive across blue's body to a double-leg takedown.

SINGLE-LEG TAKEDOWN

A single-leg takedown is the most common attack in wrestling, but because it is used so frequently, many wrestlers are adept at defending against it. The key to success with this move is to be quick and aggressive. Just as with the double-leg takedown, you launch your attack with a penetration step. Take the step toward the side you are attacking. For example, if you are attacking your opponent's left side, step to the outside of his left leg with your right foot. Keep your chin up, your back straight, and your hips low. Keep your elbows in tight to your hips until you are within range of grabbing his leg (Photo 18). See Chapter 7 for more details about a single-leg finish.

Once you have shot in and gained control of his leg, use the power from your hips to lift the leg into the air to throw your opponent off balance. You can now use the leg to drive him to the mat.

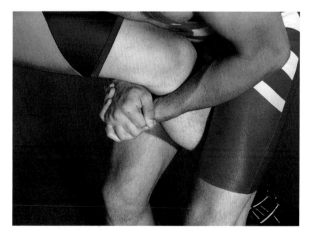

18. In a single-leg takedown, keep your elbows tight into your hips while you clasp your opponent's leg with your hands. The top hand is palm down. The knees are pinching together with the feet wide apart.

Inside Tie-up to a Single-Leg Takedown

In Photos 19 through 22, red goes from an inside tie-up to a single-leg takedown.

19. Red has an inside tie-up. Red changes his level by dropping his hips, and his weight shifts to his left leg.

20. Red then steps toward his opponent's left foot, driving down to his knee.

21. Red's back leg comes up quickly, while his shoulder drives downward into his opponent's thigh. Red's right hand is palm down in back of his opponent's knee, while is left hand is palm up.

22. Red drives off his left foot while pushing up to his feet.

Two-on-One Hold to a Single-Leg Takedown

Here is an additional move in which a wrestler goes from a two-on-one hold to a single-leg takedown (Photos 23 and 24).

23. Red moves his left hand from the triceps to the right wrist of blue so that both hands are on blue's left wrist.

24. When blue pulls up, red reaches down to grab blue's left knee. Then red drives into the leg, keeping his back straight and head up.

HIGH-CROTCH MOVES

With the high-crotch move, you attack your opponent's hips rather than his legs. This is a powerful penetration move that requires a quick finish. To set up this move, use your hand-fighting skills so that you can create an angle to get in close. Penetrate with a lead step. If your attacking your opponent's left hip, step in with your left foot. Keep your chin up as you move in, and lower your hips below his hip level. Shoot the inside arm high around the bottom of his butt, while keeping your shoulder in your opponent's hip and your head tight to his side (Photo 24).

If your opponent is leaning into you, he will go down with this initial move, but if he doesn't, you can quickly switch to a double-leg takedown, driving across your opponent (Photo 25).

24, 25. Demonstrating a high-crotch move, blue reaches high and keeps his head and shoulder in tight to red's hip. As red starts to go down, blue quickly lifts him and drives him toward the mat.

Here are some additional high-crotch takedowns.

Basic Two-on-One to a High-Crotch Takedown

Below is a basic two-on-one hold that leads to a high-crotch takedown (Photos 26 through 29).

26. Red's left hand controls blue's right triceps, while red's right hand controls his wrist. Red's left foot steps to the left as he runs blue's elbow forward and down to the right.

27. Red releases blue's right wrist and continues to pass blue's elbow down and across with his left hand. Red's right hand grabs behind blue's right knee as he takes a big step to the right of blue's foot. Red's hand is driving into blue's rib cage.

28. As red continues to drive across blue, his head moves to blue's lower rib area. Red's right knee drives down to the mat, while his left hand wraps deep behind the thigh. Red's right shoulder is tight against blue's hip.

29. Red's trail leg comes up fast. Red drives his shoulder down and across, keeping blue's weight off him.

Inside Tie-Up to a High-Crotch Takedown

52 Here is an inside tie-up that leads to a basic high-crotch takedown (Photos 30 through 33).

30. Red's left hand controls blue's right arm with an inside tie.

31. Red pulls down to the right while changing his level. As red changes his level, his chest touches his own thigh and red penetrates with his right foot.

32. Red's right hand grabs behind blue's right knee, which red pulls toward him as he drives toward the leg.

33. Red's right knee should hit the mat between blue's feet. Red's right shoulder is in blue's groin, his hips are in, he has a straight back, and his right ear is pushing across. Red's left leg comes up fast, so it can be used to drive across blue and downward.

Faking a High-Crotch Move to a Single-Leg Takedown

Here the offensive wrestler (red) fakes a high-crotch move to set himself up for a single-leg takedown. While his opponent is responding, he goes for his real goal (Photos 34 through 37).

34. Red uses his left hand to control blue's right triceps. His right hand controls blue's right wrist.

35. Red steps back with his left foot and to the left, while passing elbows downward to the right. This sets up an attack to blue's right side.

36. Blue reacts by stepping his right foot back to keep his balance, which leaves his left foot open to an attack.

37. Red changes his level and steps towards blue's left foot, driving in to a single-leg takedown.

FIREMAN'S CARRY

The fireman's carry (Photos 38 to 41) is a combination of upper body and leg attacks that can be used effectively with high-crotch moves.

38. Red reaches inside with his left hand and controls blue's wrist with his right hand. Red knocks blue off balance with a fake shot or a snap.

39. Red penetrates with his right foot, driving down to both knees. Red pulls his opponent's left arm over the top of red's head and pulls it in tight against his side. Red's own right arm is between blue's legs and wrapped tightly around blue's right hip. Red straightens his body by extending upward in order to bring blue's feet off the mat.

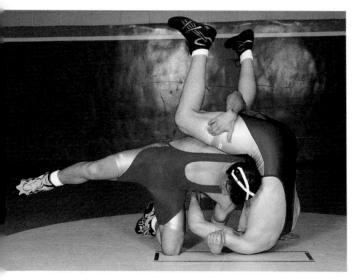

40. Red dumps blue to the mat by pulling down with his left arm and upward with the right arm. Red has to make sure he doesn't sit on his left hip, because he could easily be pulled to his back from that position.

41. Red sits to his right hip and pulls blue's left arm tight. Red brings his own right arm across blue's chest.

DUCKUNDER

The penetration step for a duckunder is a rotating shot in which you pull the opponent over you. You step in with your outside foot, hit on your inside knee, and come up quickly. It is common to start with a collar tie-up with inside control. Force his arm into his body, and your opponent naturally reacts by pulling his arm back up. As soon as he does this, you should lower your hips, step in with your outside foot, and duck your head under his arm. Once you are under your opponent's arm, lift your eyes to the ceiling and raise your head. Pull his head to the mat and reach for his far hip, and step across your opponent's body. The duckunder is shown in Photos 42 through 46.

44. Red steps his right foot across blue's body. Red steps left and secures the left hip by reaching tight into blue's groin. Red's right arm reaches across blue's chest, and red pulls down on blue's left trapezius muscle.

42. Red has inside control with his left hand. His head is next to his inside control side, and his stance is slightly staggered.

45. Red pops his hips out as he pulls down with his right arm and up with the left.

43. As blue rotates his right arm to the inside, red brings his own left arm back against blue's hip. At the same time, red rotates his head to his opponent's right hip and steps with his left leg.

46. Red continues to pull down hard with the right arm, bringing blue to his back.

SNAP-DOWN

The snap-down is very effective in turning an opponent's attack into points in your favor. Wrestlers score many points on snap-downs; it is the most effective takedown. It is low-risk and can open up your leg attacks.

As your opponent steps toward your center, lower your level and block the attack with your head and hands. Quickly move your right hand to the top of your opponent's neck, and use your left hand to take control of his right upper arm. Using a circular motion, snap down the head and the arm at the same time until he falls to the mat. Once your opponent is on the mat, make a move to spin behind him to take control. In Photos 47 to 51, red demonstrates a snap-down to a front headlock.

Defense to a Snap-Down. When your opponent is trying to pull a snap-down on you, keep your body completely square to him and drive toward him. This is called *stalking your opponent*. It helps to keep you offensive rather than defensive.

47. Red's left hand controls the inside tie, and his right hand controls the wrist. His forehead is pressing into blue's temple.

48. Red's right hand releases the wrist and snaps blue's neck downward, with the right elbow pointed down to the mat. Red pulls his left arm in and downward. His hips and center of gravity move forward.

49. Red transfers his weight to his left leg as he pulls blue forward and down to the mat. Red's right shoulder makes contact with blue's right trapezius muscle.

50. Red circles to the left as his head replaces the left hand that was on blue's triceps. Red's right hand comes over blue's head until the right elbow is positioned at the top of blue's head. His right arm cannot be controlled by blue's left hand.

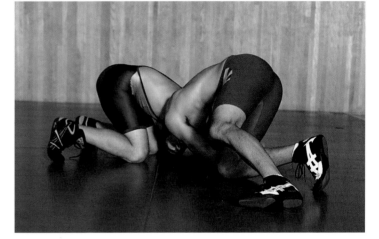

51. Red uses his left hand to grab blue's right ankle. Red's right hand pulls down and inward. Red's head is by the bottom rib as he drives blue while pulling the head and ankle together.

58

COMMON COUNTERMOVES

When your opponent attacks you, the first thing you must do is stop his hold and then counterattack. Concentrating on scoring off your opponent's attack is important.

Sprawl

A good stance is your best defense against an attack. A common defense is called the sprawl. A sprawl works well when your legs or hips are being attacked. To sprawl, thrust one hip into your opponent, toward the mat, and force your legs out behind you to try to prevent your opponent from holding your leg (Photos 52 and 53). Your hands should be on your opponent's head or around his waist, pushing him down to the mat. Ideally, your opponent will be too extended to lock his hands. Regardless, stay square to your opponent with all your weight on him. You should be thinking that this is an offensive position for you.

52, 53. Blue sprawls his legs backwards to escape from red's leg hold.

Crossface

A crossface can be used to counter a high-crotch or double-leg attack. With the opponent's head on the outside of your leg, reach across the face and grab the far triceps muscle on your opponent's arm. Reach for his ankle with your other hand and lift the leg upward until he falls on his shoulder.

Single-Leg Defense

One of the more common attacks is a single-leg takedown; a common countermove is to square your hips, shown in Photos 54 through 58.

55. Red quickly replaces his right hand with his left hand and uses the right hand to wrap around blue's waist. Red keeps his weight down as he moves blue forward and to the left.

54. Blue shoots in to secure a single leg. Red uses his right hand to push blue's head down below his hip.

56. Red turns his left hip down over blue's head and keeps his weight down by his feet so blue doesn't come underneath him. Red's right hand is locked around blue's waist.

57. Red arches his back and grabs the inside of blue's right ankle. As he moves to the left, his right knee moves in a circular motion away from blue, putting pressure on him. Red keeps his hips square to blue as he moves around him.

58. When blue releases the hold on the leg, red continues to move to the left, keeping his knees away from blue and keeping his weight down on blue's upper body. Red's left leg will scoop blue's right leg to replace red's left hand, which is holding blue's ankle.

FINISHING HOLDS

earning how to take down your opponent is very important. In order to score points, you must be able to finish your attacks. Finishing holds make the difference between winning and losing, so this is an area in which all levels of wrestlers must put forth a lot of energy.

In this phase of wrestling, it is important to keep pressure on your opponent, keeping him off balance. This will fatigue your opponent, allow you to remain offensive, and let you attack with your finishing holds.

MUSCLE MEMORY

The best way to perfect your finishing holds is through extensive drilling. The purpose for doing a great deal of drilling in wrestling is to develop muscle memory. Developing muscle memory means you must do something over and over, so that when you're physically tired, you're body naturally knows how to react. Muscle memory will help you to learn how to keep your opponent moving and on the defensive. As you gain experi-ence over time, your actions and reactions on the mat should become as natural as getting out of bed in the morning. A wrestler must always have an answer to an attack. You have to have one or two trustworthy holds so that you can always score. You should be thinking that whatever move or hold he has on you, it is not as good as what you have to counter with. Focus on what hold you're going to put on your opponent, not what move he is going to put on you. Here is a look at some of the basic finishing holds.

HIGH-CROTCH FINISHES

High-Crotch Drive across to a Double-Leg Takedown

Photos 1 through 4 show red executing a high-crotch drive that results in a double-leg takedown.

1. Red shoots in for a high-crotch move and puts his weight on his right knee and left foot. His left hand moves around blue's thigh above the right hand, which is behind the back of blue's knee. Red's back is straight and his head drives across blue.

2. Red drives up to his right foot, keeping his hips underneath him. Red's right knee blocks blue's left knee as his right hand pulls blue's leg.

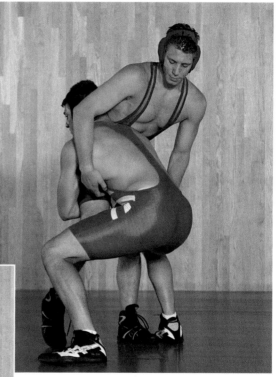

3. Red then pinches blue's legs together as red drives across with his elbows held against his hips and his shoulder down.

4. Red lifts blue for a double-leg takedown.

High-Crotch Finish from the Butt

Photos 5 through 9 show a high-crotch finish from the butt.

5. Red has a high-crotch position from his knee. He pivots over his right knee, which is placed directly under his opponent. He drives his shoulder into blue's hip as he moves his left foot in a circular motion back to the right.

6. Red drops his shoulder into blue's groin and posts his left hand. Red drops his shoulder and right hip to the mat. His right hand releases the leg and rests on the mat beside his right hip.

7. Red grabs blue's small toe with his left hand.

8. With his left arm straight, holding blue's toe and his right arm behind him on the mat, red lifts blue's leg and rests it on his left thigh, which he just raised by stepping on his left foot.

9. Red's right arm moves across blue's left leg to secure the takedown. Red keeps his body extended onto blue, with his shoulder tight and hips down.

High-Crotch Finish, Bringing the Leg Out

Photos 10 through 14 show a high-crotch finish in which the opponent's leg is brought out to topple him to the mat.

10, 11. Red is in a basic high-crotch position. He drives across blue and stands up on his feet. Blue pushes him away to try to loosen the hold on his hips.

12. Red goes to a full squat and brings his head along his opponent's hip to his thigh. Red circles slightly to his right, pivoting off his right foot. Red grabs blue's left heel with his left hand.

13. Red shifts his weight over his hips and brings blue's left leg up as he circles back to the left. With his right hand placed in the back of blue's knee, red pulls it forward. Red has his weight on his left foot so he can block, or step in with his instep, in front of blue's left shinbone and pull him forward.

14. As blue's weight moves forward and down to his hands, red brings his left hand to meet his right hand and moves his right hand to the front of blue's left thigh. Red drives across him as red brings his elbows into his hips.

SINGLE-LEG FINISHES

Single-Leg Finish Holds

A single-leg finish is shown in Photos 15 through 19.

16. Red drives upward while locking his knees together; his feet are apart. Red extends his arms between his legs as though hiking a football.

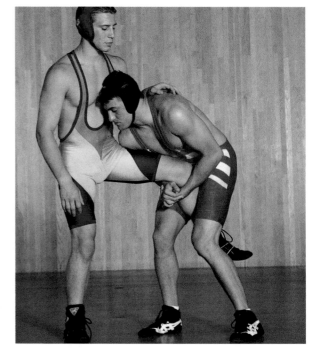

15. Red's right knee supports his weight as he puts pressure on his opponent's ribs.

17. Red pivots over his right foot while moving to the right. His right leg is supporting blue's weight. Red is in a full squat, with his weight down and back. Red pushes down with his right hand as he turns blue's knee toward the mat. Red circles to the right, steps over blue's leg with his left leg, transfers his right hand above the knee, and brings his left hand to blue's shoelaces.

18. In one motion, with his chest against blue's calf, red brings the leg up with the heel in red's hip and the knee by red's chest. Red pulls up and in with his right hand, transfers his weight to his left leg, and blocks behind his calf with his right leg. From here, red brings blue's foot to his left hip while pulling and blocking at the same time.

19. Once blue lands on the mat, red pulls blue's leg in and will crawl up his leg, replacing his right hand with the left.

Thigh-Pry Single-Leg Finish

Photos 20 through 23 show a thigh-pry single-leg finish.

20. Starting from the basic single-leg takedown position, red has his head up so that his forehead is in blue's rib cage. Red's shoulder is driving downward into blue's thigh. Red's right hand is palm down, interlocking with his left hand.

21. Red's right hand releases his left hand and it moves to blue's mid-thigh. Red's right shoulder drops to the base of blue's butt. Red's motion is circular as red pivots over his right toe.

22. Red continues to move in a circular motion as his right arm is locked straight. His left hand has a very tight grip on blue's left leg.

23. When blue's weight is on his hands, red transfers his right hand around the outside of blue's leg. Red drives hard into blue, keeping his shoulder below blue's butt.

Low-Level Single-Leg Finish

Here we see red executing a low-level single-leg takedown (Photos 24 through 28).

24. Red works on getting an angle and then attacks blue's left leg. Red drives his right shoulder into blue's upper left thigh. Red's hands are directly below him, touching the mat. Red's head is pushing up and into blue, while he pivots on his hands in a circular motion.

25, 26. Red circles until his right knee comes behind blue's left ankle. Red's weight is back toward his hips. Red's right knee moves about 6" (15 cm) to the left. That locks out blue's hips so he cannot square his body.

27. Red moves his right hand to blue's left thigh. Red's left hand moves to blue's left ankle, and red steps up to the left foot to pull blue's leg into his hip. Red shifts his weight toward his right hip so that blue can't pull him forward. Driving his shoulder into blue's left butt muscle, red pinches down on the leg that is on his thigh so blue can't kick out of the hold.

28. Red's left hand transfers from the ankle to the left thigh. Red's right hand moves to the right ankle, and he keeps his shoulder low to drive into blue.

Single-Leg Finish Coming Underneath

Photos 29 through 33 show a single-leg finish in which red comes underneath his opponent.

29. Blue squares his hips, taking pressure off red's right side. Red steps up with his right foot and posts with his left hand.

30. Red turns his head up and to the right as he raises his right hand. Red slides his left knee forward until it is underneath blue. Red moves his heels quickly to protect them and to maintain this position. He drives his weight into blue to throw him off balance.

31. Red pulls down with his right arm on the back of blue's left leg. Red's left arm reaches to the ankle of the same leg. Red swings the leg down and to his left as he sits blue to his left hip.

32. Red pulls blue's left ankle toward him with his left arm. Red drives his shoulders into blue's groin, locking his hips into place.

33. Red hooks blue's heel with his left leg, and pulls the leg toward him. Red pops his head out to blue's right hip and turns blue's hips toward the mat.

WRESTLING EQUIPS YOU WITH LIFE SKILLS

KENDALL CROSS

"Winning was the carrot that was out in front of me. Winning is what made me a motivated wrestler," says Kendall Cross, a 1996 Olympic gold medalist.

Kendall Cross dabbled with wrestling for five years in a youth program in Billings, Montana, until he decided to take it more seriously when he was in high school. He was a 115-pound state champion at Oklahoma's Mustang High School in 1985. From there he went to Oklahoma State, where he was a three-time All-American wrestler and a 126-pound NCAA Champion in 1989.

"When it comes to wrestling styles, I am a finesse wrestler. I am not very muscular or fast, so I have to be very technique-based. I prefer to take the path of least resistance," he says.

Kendall Cross is a very intelligent wrestler. He observes, "I am not a genetically inclined athlete. I won a lot of matches based on strategy. I really used my head. I was definitely in shape and the technique side of things was in place, but I always stuck with my strategy."

The skill sets that Kendall Cross feels are needed to be a good wrestler include commitment and focus. "Those are the two things that transfer out of wrestling and into life and business. Seeing it all pay off was huge for me," he says, adding: "Now I feel like I can do anything. I have a higher standard for myself because of wrestling."

Kendall Cross realizes how hard it is to always give 100% in practices and competition. "Young wrestlers have to realize that there is a delayed gratification. You really have to work hard for something that doesn't always pay off immediately. It can be difficult to balance nutrition and training for a distant match."

He encourages wrestlers to stick with it. There is a much larger picture with wrestling. "This sport, like other individual sports, has the opportunity to teach you about life. You have to learn to rely on yourself."

MAT WRESTLING: TOP AND BOTTOM POSITIONS

8

Getting your opponent down to the mat is only half the battle in wrestling. Mat wrestling from the top and bottom positions can lead to many points in a match. This chapter features breakdowns, some basic turns to get your opponent onto his back, and some basic ways to defend yourself when you are caught on the bottom.

BREAKDOWNS

After you successfully score a takedown and gain top control, the first thing you should seek to do is control your opponent's hips, force his weight onto his hands, and extend his body so he is forced to carry your weight on his back. If you are very physical and you use good technique from the top position, you can exhaust your opponent and frustrate him. Here are three basic breakdowns to try: the spiral ride, tight waist with an arm chop, and the tight waist with ankle control.

The Spiral Ride

The goal in using the spiral ride is to get your opponent flat on the mat by putting a lot of weight on his upper body and driving forward in a circular motion. To create that circular motion, hook your arm underneath your opponent's near-side armpit so that your hand is clasping either his shoulder or behind his neck (Photo 1). Drive your forehead into the back of your opponent's head, driving it downward (Photo 2) so that he ends up with his head down and his butt up. Your other arm comes over his back and into his inside thigh. Make sure your foot is about 6" (15 cm) away from your opponent's hand so that there is a heavy pressure forward, while you pry out both sides to flatten him (Photo 3).

1, 2, and 3. Red puts heavy pressure on blue's upper back while hooking his left hand under blue's armpit. Red's right hand reaches to blue's inner thigh. Red steps his left foot up near blue's left hand, rises up on his toes, and drives blue forward in a circular motion until he is flat on the mat.

Tight Waist with Arm Chop

Photos 4 to 6 show the tight waist with arm chop move.

4. Red has his right hand tightly around blue's waist.

5. Red's right knee is driving into blue's butt. Red's left hand hooks blue's lower biceps, pulling it with a twisting motion into blue's waist. Red drives with his hips and legs forward and to the right, trapping blue's left arm to his side.

6. Red drives blue down to the mat and gets his weight on top of him.

Tight Waist with Ankle Control

Photos 7 and 8 show the tight waist with ankle control move. The wrestlers started in the referee's position, as in Photo 4.

7. Red moves his left hand from blue's left elbow down to the waist. Red's right hand moves from blue's waist to blue's right ankle.

8. Blue uses his left shoulder to drive into red's lower back. As red drives blue forward, red lifts the ankle up and to the left.

TURNS

The main objective in wrestling is to pin your opponent, and the only way to pin him is to turn him onto his back. A great time to turn your opponent is right after a takedown, when you have top control and he has lost his focus. Some basic ways to turn your opponent are: leg and arm turks, the crossface cradle, the overhead cradle, the half nelson with wrist control, the arm bar with wrist control, and the overhead cradle (also known as the near-side cradle).

Leg and Arm Turks

A turk is a move in which you hook and control your opponent's leg above the knee. A leg turk is done with your leg; an arm turk is done with your arm. A turk is the most effective turn from

a double-leg takedown or a high-crotch take-down. The main objective with a leg turk is to control your opponent's hips so that they are trapped and facing up toward the ceiling. Once his hips are controlled, you can turn his upper body. This is a very common turn at college and international levels, and can be very effective at the high school level if properly learned.

Leg and arm turks can be used to maintain control of your opponent when you have him down on the mat. If your opponent is in the bottom position and is on his bottom hip, you should seek to control his bottom leg by hooking it with your arm as you move to get back points (Photo 9).

With the leg turk shown here, hold one ankle with your hand and pull your opponent's other leg away with your leg (Photo 10).

9. Red uses his left hand to lift the inside of blue's left thigh by the knee. Red's right shoulder drives into blue's body, while red's right arm either does a crossface, an arm bar, or an overhead cradle. The key is to drive and lift the bottom leg with the left arm.

10. Red controls blue's hip that is toward the mat. When blue turns to his left hip, red hooks blue's left ankle with his left heel. Red pulls the heel toward his head, until he can get the back of blue's left knee against the back of his own knee. Red holds blue's right ankle down onto the mat to gain control of his left leg. This creates the opportunity to split the legs. Red lifts the left leg forward and toward the ceiling as he drives with his right leg.

Crossface Cradle

80 You can use the crossface cradle if your opponent is flat on the mat (Photos 11 through 15).

11. Blue breaks red down to the mat. He blocks red's left elbow with his right hand. Blue's right forearm is across red's cheekbone and mouth, with his hand grabbing high on his triceps. Blue uses his right shoulder to force red's upper body down into the mat as he pulls the triceps in to his body, which forces red's left shoulder to turn in to the mat.

12. Blue keeps pressure on red's upper body by placing his left hand on the mat behind red's left knee.

13. Blue steps up with his right foot and bends red by bringing red's head to the knee.

14. Blue connects his hands. He slides his right knee under red's left hip. Blue runs red straight back over his inside thigh.

15. Blue finishes this hold with his forehead at red's left temple and his right knee just below the bottom rib on the left side.

Half Nelson with Wrist Control

In Photos 16 through 18, blue demonstrates the half nelson with wrist control.

16. Blue breaks red down to his stomach. Blue's right arm is under red's arm and his right hand is on the back of red's head. Blue's left hand grabs red's left wrist.

17. Blue makes a fist with his right hand, and red's forehead is on top of that hand. Blue flexes his forearm and drives with his legs so that he ends up chest to chest with red. Blue sinks his half nelson hold deep, so that his elbow is behind red's head.

18. Blue keeps his head up while he is pinning red.

Arm Bar with Wrist Control

The arm bar with wrist control is shown in Photos 19 through 22.

19. Blue has the crook of his right elbow in alignment with red's elbow. Blue's chest is tight against red's triceps and blue's left hand is underneath and holding red's left arm.

20. Blue slides his left knee forward while he pulls up and back on red's right arm. Blue's hand is making a fist.

21. Blue brings his right leg forward so that his hips are squared to the mat. Blue drives red's right shoulder into red's right ear. Blue has to be careful, because red could escape by bringing his right arm forward, or could sit up when the weight comes off his head. Blue sits his left hip down towards the mat next to red's head and holds the wrist in place with his left hand.

22. Blue pushes into the middle of red's back, bringing red's shoulders down against the mat.

Overhead Cradle or Near-Side Cradle

The overhead cradle is shown in Photos 23 through 25.

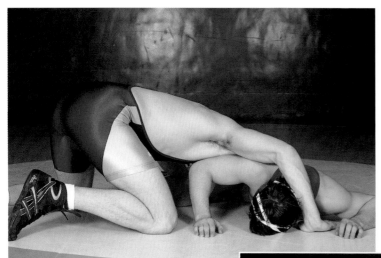

23. Blue has his right arm over red's head.

24. Blue drives with his legs as he brings his hands together.

25. Blue drives red to his back. It is important that blue keep his right elbow facing down toward the mat while he keeps red's head down.

BOTTOM POSITION

There are several keys to wrestling from the bottom position. The most important thing is to keep your hips moving and underneath you. Use your elbows to assist you in fighting for hand control. Make sure you are constantly trying to put pressure back onto the opponent.

Defending against a Tight Waist with Ankle Control

Defending a tight waist with ankle control is shown in Photos 26 through 29.

28. Blue pushes back up to his feet, driving off his front foot. Blue extends red's right arm, pulling it down and forward, as well as pushing back with his upper body.

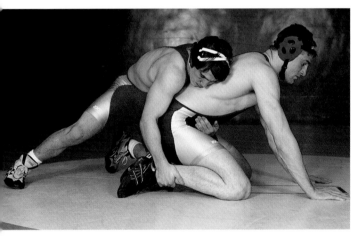

26. Blue feels red grab his right ankle.

27. Blue rotates over his right foot and grabs the wrist that holds that ankle. Blue pushes off his right foot, extending his leg.

29. Blue raises his opponent's arm and twists his hips to spin.

Switch

The switch moves you from underneath to on top (Photos 30 to 33). The wrestlers started in the referee's position, with red's right arm on blue's waist (see Photo 4).

30. Blue rotates his right knee up as he brings his left hand over his right hand.

31. Blue pushes off his bottom hand and rotates to his right hip.

32. Blue scoots his hips down into the mat and away from red. Blue grabs red's wrist, which is around his waist, with his left hand. His right hand reaches under red's right knee.

33. Blue takes red's wrist off his waist and places it down on the mat. Blue drives into red, placing his left hand on red's far ankle.

Stand-up

Photos 34 through 38 demonstrate the stand-up.

34. Blue shifts his weight back onto his hips.

35. Blue throws his left arm across his body as he catches red's left wrist with his right hand. At the same time, blue steps up with his left foot at a 90-degree angle.

36. Blue pushes back with his left foot, keeping his hips low. Blue grabs red's wrist with his left hand, and extends it down and forward.

37. Blue places red's left arm behind blue's hip as blue pops his hips away and pushes back with his upper body. Blue raises his right arm into the air. Blue drops his right hip and twists, bringing his right arm down the right trapezius and through the middle of red's body.

38. Blue creates a distance between himself and red.

Defending the Half Nelson

Photos 39 and 40 show a defense to a half nelson.

39. The half nelson.

40. Red looks away from the half nelson and peels away blue's hand from his head. Red will hold onto that hand and slide his hips forward.

Change-Over: Defense to a Spiral Ride

Photos 41 to 44 show a defense to a spiral ride.

41. Blue rotates his right knee upward, keeping his right foot in place.

43. Blue's back is straight and his legs are at a 90° angle. Blue brings his right hand across to red's left hand; blue's right elbow is pinching down, trapping red's right wrist. Blue uses both hands to force red's hand down to his hip.

42. Blue rotates around to his bottom hip, posting his left foot and his right hand. Blue pushes off his left foot and right hand as he replaces his right hip with his right knee.

44. Blue pushes back with his left foot over his right foot with his hips low. Blue's left hand and elbow are inside red's. Blue raises his right hand straight up, while twisting and dropping his hips to the left. Blue does not move left or right, he just drops and spins. His back should be pushing into red's as his hips pop forward, creating space between himself and his opponent.

GLOSSARY

Action: Referee's command to the wrestlers to start wrestling.

Alignment: The way the wrestler's head, shoulders, hips, knees, and feet are lined up vertically.

Ankle ride: Attempt to control or break down an opponent on the bottom by grasping and lifting his ankle.

Arm control: Controlling the opponent's arms.

Attack: The offensive moves a wrestler makes in competition.

Base of support: The parts of the body that are supporting the wrestler's weight on the mat.

Block: A wrestler's attempt to prevent an opponent from shooting in.

Body lock: A hold in which a wrestler locks arms around the torso of his opponent and tries to take him to the mat.

Body throw: A move in which a wrestler locks arms around the body of his opponent and throws him to the mat.

Break down: (v.) To flatten an opponent to the mat on his stomach or side when the opponent starts from the bottom position.

Breakdown: (n.) A move in which the top wrestler flattens an opponent to the mat on the opponent's stomach or side when the opponent is in the bottom position.

Bridge: The arched position a wrestler adopts, with his back facing the mat, supporting himself on his head, elbows and feet, to avoid having his shoulders touch the mat.

Center: Starting area in the center of the mat.

Center of gravity: Location at which the mass (weight) of a body is concentrated.

Central circle: The small inner circle of the wrestling mat.

Central wrestling area: The circle on a wrestling mat between the central circle and the passivity zone.

Chicken wing: Illegal pinning combination in which the nearside arm is hooked and barred across the back.

Creating an angle: Making a move to try to attack from the side when you and your opponent are both on your feet.

Double-leg takedown: A move in which a wrestler takes down his opponent by holding both the opponent's legs with his arms and tackling him.

Duckunder: (n.) A takedown from a tie-up in which the offensive wrestler pulls his opponent's arm back up over his head and ducks his head under the arm to unbalance the opponent.

Escape: Move in which the bottom wrestler breaks free of the top wrestler's control.

Fall (or pin): (n). Act of forcing an opponent's shoulders to the mat for a certain number of seconds.

FILA: *Fédération Internationale des Luttes Associées,* which means International Federation of Associated Wrestling Styles. The international governing body of wrestling.

Fireman's carry: A takedown that combines an upper body lock on an arm and a center-step leg attack through the crotch so that the opponent is thrown to his back.

Folkstyle: (1) Any local style of wrestling. (2) The style of wrestling primarily used in the United States in youth programs, high schools, and colleges. Also called collegiate or scholastic wrestling.

Freestyle: The international cousin to folkstyle. A form of wrestling in which wrestlers may use their arms, bodies, and legs and may hold opponents above or below the waist. Similar to folkstyle.

Front headlock: An upper body throw using an overhead hold and a back step.

Greco-Roman: A traditional international form of wrestling in which wrestlers may use only their arms and upper bodies to attack and may hold only those parts of their opponents that are above the waist.

Hand fighting: Competition in which two standing wrestlers are constantly moving their hands, trying to gain control.

High-crotch move: A takedown move from an outside step in which the opponent's hip strength is neutralized long enough to complete the move.

Inside leg: Leg closest to opponent's body.

Inside penetration step. *See* Penetration step.

Inside tie-up: A hand-fighting move in which one wrestler locks up his arm inside his opponent's arm.

Lead foot: The forward foot in a staggered stance.

Lead knee: The forward knee in a stance.

Nearfall: Position in which a wrestler is close to getting pinned: his shoulders are less than 4 inches (10 cm) from the mat and at an angle to the mat of 45 degrees or less. Points are awarded for a nearfall.

Neutral position: Starting position at the beginning of a match, in which both wrestlers are on their feet in their stances, facing each other but not touching, and neither has control.

Passivity: Stalling and avoiding combat; adopting a "negative" approach to a bout by trying to avoid the action.

Passivity zone: A 39" (1 m) wide band inside the edge of the mat.

Penetration step: A step made by the offensive wrestler either between the defensive wrestler's legs (inside penetration step) or outside (outside penetration step) in order to gain a takedown.

Pin: Another term for a fall.

Posting: A moved used from the offensive or defensive position. Defensively, a wrestler locks his arm to hold off his opponent. Offensively, a wrestler pushes up on his opponent's arm under the elbow to clear the arm to shoot in.

Protection area: Out-of-bounds area of the mat, beyond the passivity zone.

Referee's position: The starting position on the mat in which the bottom wrestler has his hands and knees on the mat and the top wrestler is kneeling behind him with one hand on his arm and one arm around his opponent's waist.

Reversal: Action in which the bottom wrestler reverses his position and comes to the top position in control.

Setup: Movements, level changes, or fakes that cause the opponent to move into a position that leaves him open to an attack.

Shooting: Attack by the offensive wrestler of the defensive wrestler's legs in order to gain a takedown.

Snap-down: A takedown, usually used as a counter, in which the opponent's head is directed down toward the mat.

Single-leg takedown: A move in which a wrestler takes down his opponent by lifting the opponent's leg with his arm.

Singlet: A close-fitting nylon or spandex one-piece uniform that a wrestler wears for competitions.

Spiral ride: A breakdown from the top position in which the wrestler tries to flatten his opponent to the mat by prying the opponent's base position apart.

Sprawl: A counter to a leg attack, in which the

legs are thrown straight back, away from the opponent.

Squared stance: A defensive stance in which the wrestler's toes and knees are aligned and shoulders-width apart.

Staggered stance: An offensive stance in which one foot is in front of the other.

Stalling: Intentionally delaying the match. If a wrestler receives two warnings from the referee for stalling, he is penalized one point.

Takedown: Act of taking an opponent from a standing position to the mat to gain control. This move is awarded two points.

Technical points: Points scored during the match for actions and holds.

Tie-up: A type of lock or hold in which a wrestler in the neutral position attempts to control the opponent's upper body while looking for an opening for a takedown.

Turk: Leg or arm hold used against an opponent that involves twisting around and lifting the opponent's leg.

Trail leg: The back leg in a staggered stance.

Two-on-one: Hold in which a wrestler controls one arm of his opponent's by having two hands on it.

INDEX

ABOUT THE AUTHORS

Tom Ryan

When Tom was a youngster and saw a high school wrestling match for the first time, he knew it was the sport for him. He was instantly drawn to wrestling because it is so appealing to athletes of all shapes, sizes, and abilities.

He wrestled at Syracuse University and at the University of Iowa under Coach Dan Gable. He was a 2-time Big Ten Champion, 2-time All-American, an NCAA finalist, and a member of two national championship teams at Iowa. Later he became an assistant wrestling coach at the University of Indiana.

In 1995, he became the head wrestling coach at Hofstra University, where he has coached 18 East Coast Wrestling Association (ECWA) champions, as of the writing of this book. He sent 25 wrestlers from his program to the NCAA Championships as well, with four earning All-American honors. In 1998, 2000, and 2001, he was named ECWA Coach of the Year. In 1998 and 2001 Tom was named New York State Coach of the Year. He is married to Lynette Ryan and they have four children: Jordan, Jake, Teague, and MacKenzie.

Julie Sampson

Julie is a freelance writer living in Fort Salonga, Long Island. She has reported on amateur sports for *Newsday* and other publications, and from 1988-91 was sports editor of Imprint Newspapers in West Hartford.

A 1988 graduate of Springfield College, Julie was a soccer player and the editor of the college newspaper. She coached high school soccer and softball in Connecticut and continues to coach youth soccer on Long Island. Julie is married to John Sampson and they have two children, Troy and Sheila.